# DYNAMITE

INVENTIONS THAT CHANGED OUR LIVES

# DYNAMITE

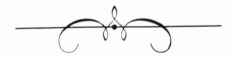

## Diana C. Gleasner

WALKER AND COMPANY  New York

**Library of Congress Cataloging in Publication Data**

Gleasner, Diana C.
  Dynamite: inventions that changed our lives.

  Includes index.
  Summary: Discusses the uses of dynamite and the
industrial and technological progress that followed its
invention in 1866 by chemical engineer Alfred Nobel.
  1. Dynamite—Juvenile literature.   2. Nobel, Alfred
Bernhard, 1833–1896—Juvenile literature.   3. Chemical
engineers—Biography—Juvenile literature.   [1. Dynamite.
2. Explosives.   3. Nobel, Alfred Bernhard, 1833–1896]
I. Title
TP285.G53   1982              662'.27              82-4801
ISBN 0-8027-6466-5                                 AACR2
ISBN 0-8027-6467-3

First published in the United States of America in 1982 by the Walker Pub-
lishing Company, Inc.

Published simultaneously in Canada by John Wiley & Sons Canada, Limited,
Rexdale, Ontario.

ISBN: 0-8027-6466-5 Tr.
      0-8027-6467-3 Reinf.

Library of Congress Catalog Card Number: 82-4801

Book designed by LENA FONG HOR

Printed in the United States of America

10   9   8   7   6   5   4   3   2   1

# CONTENTS

*Preface*                                                        vii

*Chapter 1*  GUNPOWDER:
             Forerunner of Dynamite                                9

*Chapter 2*  NITROGLYCERIN:
             Dynamite's Prime Ingredient                          16

*Chapter 3*  BLASTING OIL
             (Nitroglycerin):
             Explosive Problems                                   22

*Chapter 4*  DYNAMITE:
             Nitroglycerin Tamed                                  40

*Chapter 5*  THE NOBEL PEACE PRIZES:
             Nobel's Gift to Humanity                             58

*Index*                                                          62

*To the memory of my scientist father,*
*Delmer L. Cottle*

# PREFACE

The world would be a far different place if man had not invented dynamite. Dynamite was a tremendous source of energy that changed the shape of the earth. It gave humans power over the physical world and control over their environment.

Dynamite permitted projects of enormous scope and variety. It deepened river and harbor channels and helped build roads, bridges, tunnels, and canals. At last transportation was faster than the plodding pace of an aging horse. Because of dynamite, mining and quarrying could be done on a grand scale and incredible buried treasures—minerals, precious metals, and other natural resources—unearthed. These vast riches, once locked inside mountains, finally could be put to use by civilization.

Dynamite ushered in the industrial age and unleashed technological progress that was truly astonishing. Many of today's industries, particularly chemical, construction, and mining, owe their rapid development to this invention.

Dynamite was an exciting chapter in the evolution of explosives. The knowledge gained in its research paved the way for the awesome weapons of the nuclear age. But it also led to advances with wonderful potential for humanity—from new ways of generating power to rocket fuels that made exploration of space possible.

The dramatic discovery of dynamite in 1866 kindled the imagination of inventors who came afterwards. Suddenly, anything and everything seemed possible.

Thanks to this heritage, nothing is beyond our reach—not even travel to the farthest star.

# 1

# GUNPOWDER

*The Forerunner of Dynamite*

DYNAMITE CHANGED the face of the earth. Alfred Nobel, the inventor of this powerful explosive, owed a debt to the Chinese love of fireworks, the Arabs' experiments with guns, and an English monk's search for scientific knowledge.

The earliest-known explosives were made in China, probably as early as the 10th century. The Chinese mixed sulfur, charcoal, and saltpeter to make a powder that, when ignited, created a bright burst of fire. They used this magic mixture in fireworks, signals, and rockets. Written descriptions of royal celebrations in the 13th century report brilliant displays of shooting sparks and balls of fire amid plenty of noise. From these crude beginnings came the first gunpowder, known throughout the world as black powder.

Zero plus 8.4 seconds. In 1958 this huge underwater explosion was the greatest non-atomic blast ever fired by man.

"Huo Yao," the name the Chinese gave this explosive mixture, was later used to shoot solid fragments from bamboo tubes. Credit for the first real gun goes to the Arabs. They apparently learned about black powder from the Chinese, for in their earliest written reference to saltpeter, the Arabs called it "Chinese snow." In 1304 they used this powder to shoot arrows from bamboo tubes reinforced with iron. They were using the same principle that hurls today's spaceships into outer space. When confined explosive material is ignited, the suddenly released gases create a powerful propelling force as they expand and try to escape.

Gunpowder has been known to mankind for more than 1000 years. Although it was invented well before 1000 A.D., it wasn't until 1242 that the formula was recorded in the Western world. At that time few people could read or write, and a college education was a rare prize. The men of the church were an exception. They were encouraged to get as much learning as they could.

Roger Bacon, an English monk, was a graduate of Oxford University and had studied languages and science at the University of Paris. He had a keen interest in ancient warfare and read everything he could about the wildfire once used by the Greeks in sea battles. They had made great tongues of fire shoot from the ends of tubes carved to look like horrible beasts.

In his attempt to create wildfire, Bacon made a black powder from brimstone (sulfur) and the charcoal of young hazel twigs. One day he decided to add saltpeter to the mixture. Bacon had probably read about saltpeter while studying early Arab writings, but he could not have been prepared for the results. When he flicked a spark from his flint on the mix-

11

ture, it instantly blew up. There was a great flash of light, a shock, and a loud noise. Of the many, many experiments Bacon had tried in his lonely cell, this was surely the most startling. After the smoke had cleared and he had recovered from the blast, Roger Bacon did some serious thinking.

He was smart enough to know he had made a discovery that would rock the world. Bacon was also a religious man who wanted to do the right thing. As far as anyone knows, he was the first to write down the formula. Because he realized his discovery was dangerous and could cause great harm, he recorded it in a secret code. He thought it would be better if only people with intelligence and learning knew how to make it. They were more likely to use it for the good of humanity, less likely to use it to kill and destroy.

The code, written in Latin, was very difficult and proved to be hard to break. It was 650 years before a British army colonel cracked the code and revealed Bacon's recipe for black powder. Along with the formula Bacon had written was the warning that those who followed his instructions would bring forth "thunder and destruction."

Well before Bacon's formula was decoded, the secret of making black powder was unlocked. Between the 13th and 17th centuries the ability to produce and use this explosive spread throughout the countries of western Europe. The impact was staggering. Black powder caused nothing less than a world revolution.

Up until this invention kings could rule safely

Man-made explosives totally revolutionized warfare. (Destruction of the battleship *Maine* in Havana Harbor, 1898.)

from their well-fortified castles. All powerful land-owners could make up any rules they wanted for the lowly peasants who worked their fields. These land-lords relied on knights in armor to protect them and their interests. The system was unfair, but those who objected were quickly killed.

With gunpowder came the chance for the common man to say he had had enough. No longer were sword-waving knights the rulers of the battlefield. Warfare would never again be the same. The old

13

Iron mining was once a tedious, backbreaking process.

weapons—sword, bow and arrow, battle axe, and battering ram—were replaced by ammunition. Castles were not cannonproof any more than kings were bulletproof. A bullet didn't know or care whether a man had been born rich or poor. The humblest serf with a gun in his hand was able to stand up to royalty. The once powerless footsoldier was now feared and respected. The system of rule by royalty, which everyone thought would last forever, tumbled and fell. Thomas Carlyle, a British historian, summed up this turning point in history by saying, "Gunpowder made all men tall."

Was black powder a blessing or a curse? When it was used to kill and maim, Roger Bacon was probably stirring uncomfortably in his grave. When it was used to put the world on the road to democracy, the common man would say it was the work of heaven. There was no question it improved the lot of humanity when it was first used in mining in the 1600s. At last the knowledge of explosives was being put to peaceful use. Humans were saving themselves backbreaking labor as they broke open mountains. Before long they would be moving them.

# 2

# NITROGLYCERIN

*Dynamite's Prime Ingredient*

WE ALL OWE a debt to those who have gone before us. Inventors are especially aware of all the experiments that have paved their way. One idea builds on another. The radio was invented before television, the airplane before the spaceship. Roger Bacon probably would not have discovered black powder if he hadn't read about Chinese and Arabian experiments with fireworks and other crude forms of explosives.

Alfred Nobel gathered all the knowledge he could about explosives. All his life he questioned and experimented. His inventor's mind never accepted the idea that there was only one way to do something. There could always be improvements, better methods of solving age-old problems. Over and over he asked himself, "What if?" What if he changed the shape, lowered the temperature, mixed this with

AMERICAN METHOD OF TUNNELING

Heading-and-Bench Method, about 1840. Four crews Drilling with Double-Jacks while the Muck Gang loads out. Black Powder was the only explosive.

Black powder was a tremendous help when it came to tunneling through a mountain.

that? By answering his own questions, he was able to travel the difficult path that would lead to the discovery of dynamite.

It wasn't easy. Nobel's life was full of troubles,

17

but that didn't stop him from striving for a new and better way to do things. Alfred was a very practical man who wanted his inventions to be successful and useful. This meant he had to spend a great deal of time outside the laboratory protecting his ideas from being stolen, setting up factories, and convincing others that his products would not blow them to bits.

A lot of different scientists contributed to Nobel's discoveries. Some, like Roger Bacon, died long before Nobel was born. Others, like Ascanio Sobrero, did their work during Alfred's lifetime. Sobrero was a chemistry professor at the University of Turin in Italy. In 1846 he tried mixing sulfuric and nitric acids with glycerin, a syrupy liquid used primarily as a hand lotion. When combined at a low temperature, this mixture produced an oily yellow liquid that looked like salad oil. Sobrero could not guess his discovery would lead to a whole new group of super explosives.

What he did know was that the liquid was pretty strong stuff. Sobrero heated a single drop of nitroglycerin in a glass tube. It exploded with such violence that glass splinters cut deeply into his face and hands and wounded workers in far corners of his laboratory.

Sobrero's experiments with nitroglycerin were frightening. No one had to tell him the liquid was highly dangerous. The powerful mixture never reacted twice in the same way. It seemed to have a mind of its own. Since it was totally unpredictable,

The Boston Massacre (March 5, 1770).

Sobrero concluded it could never be controlled or used for any practical purpose. How could it ever be manufactured? And if it were, what horrors would it bring? Sobrero was a peace-loving man who saw

nothing but trouble ahead. Besides, nitroglycerin was a poison. A tiny amount placed on his tongue caused a terrible headache and made him incredibly weak all over. A few drops killed a dog in a very short time. He decided to stop experimenting with this awesome explosive.

After keeping nitroglycerin a secret for a year, Sobrero finally informed other scientists of his discovery in 1847. He warned them of its dangers and urged them to leave it alone. He stressed the fact that it was only a scientific curiosity, of no practical use. But when he shared his knowledge with others, Ascanio Sobrero gave the chemical formula for nitroglycerin to the world.

Black powder was king during the difficult days of the Revolutionary War.

Transporting black powder for use in the war effort. (Paintings by Howard Pyle in *Harper's New Monthly* magazine, July 1886.)

# 3

# BLASTING OIL
# (Nitroglycerin)

*Explosive Problems*

ALFRED NOBEL was born in 1833 in a rundown house on the outskirts of Stockholm, Sweden. He was a very weak baby who probably would have died had it not been for his mother who tenderly nursed him through one crisis after another. Of the family's eight children, only four survived infancy. Alfred's three brothers were normal boys who went to school and played outside with their friends. But Alfred spent most of his childhood in bed fighting off one illness after another.

Although he didn't attend school, Alfred was tutored at home by his mother. He read many books to pass the time and eagerly followed the progress of his father's and brothers' experiments. They were always trying something new. Alfred might have had a very boring childhood if he hadn't been born into a family of inventors.

Saltpeter refinery in the 1920s. (Saltpeter is an essential ingredient of black powder.)

The Nobels had many worries. The year Alfred was born, his father had no money to pay his bills. His seven-year-old brother sold matchsticks on the street corner trying to earn enough so his mother could buy food for supper. Mr. Nobel didn't give up hope. He was always waiting for his *next* invention, which he was sure would make them a fortune. When the Czar of Russia offered him a job designing torpedoes for the Russian Navy, Mr. Nobel left Sweden. Later, when Alfred was nine, Mr. Nobel sent for his family to join him in Russia. Finally, he had a chance to put his talents to work. For a while he made enough money for a decent living. There was even some extra for a private tutor for Alfred. Except for one year in school, that brief period of private in-

Interior of a saltpeter refinery.

struction was the extent of his formal education. He never went to college, but he learned everything he could by reading, watching, and asking questions.

The family was very close. Alfred's mother was a loving, hardworking woman who did her best to keep the family happy and comfortable despite their troubles. Alfred admired his older brothers, Robert and Ludwig. They were smart, ambitious young men determined to better themselves. Oscar Emil, his much-loved younger brother, also showed great potential.

Alfred Nobel grew up to be a lonely man. He always said the most satisfying thing a man could have was a family, but he never had one of his own. Though he did not marry, he had a long relationship with a much younger woman who acted like a spoiled child. She made impossible demands on Alfred, and wasted a great deal of his money. It annoyed her that Nobel devoted himself almost entirely to his work. He had no hobbies, nor was he interested in relaxing or being entertained. Although his health was poor throughout his life, he was able to do an astonishing amount of work. Because his business demanded a great deal of travel, he crisscrossed Europe and even spent some time in the United States. He used to say, "My home is where I work and I work everywhere."

Alfred's work soon took him into the field of explosives, but he did not find out about nitroglycerin directly from the Italian Ascanio Sobrero. He learned about it while living in Russia. There he watched a professor of chemistry put a pool of the oily liquid on an anvil and strike it with a hammer. The blow caused a small explosion. He hit the oil again in a different spot and produced another blast. Alfred Nobel was fascinated. He, his father, and his brothers had been working on explosives. They realized this strange exploding oil was an important discovery.

Many problems remained to be solved. They had to find a way to explode it that would work every time. They had to make it safe to manufacture, store, and transport from one place to another. Otherwise, it was just an exciting laboratory experiment to fire the imagination. Alfred immediately began to work on solutions. For more than a dozen years nitroglycerin had been something for scientists to wonder about. It was time to put it to good use.

The first problem was to make the oil explode

Alfred Nobel (1833–1896), inventor of dynamite.

consistently. Men who tested it in the field said it couldn't possibly be used for blasting. It had plenty of force, but it wasn't reliable. Often when they lit the fuse, nitroglycerin burned instead of exploding.

Alfred tried mixing nitroglycerin with gunpowder. That worked a little better but was not the answer. Next he tried floating a gunpowder cartridge on the explosive oil. There had to be a better way to set off a mighty blast.

In 1862 Nobel worked on a series of experiments in a water-filled ditch. They were all based on his belief that the best way to explode nitroglycerin consistently was to use one kind of explosive to ignite another. He filled a glass tube with the volatile oil, corked it, and inserted the tube into a tin container filled with gunpowder. After lighting the fuse to the gunpowder, he shoved the whole thing under water.

The result? In Nobel's own words, "A very sharp shaking of the ground and a spout . . ." The trembling earth and tall column of water that erupted from the ditch signalled success. The gunpowder had set off the nitroglycerin! Now if he could only prove this method would work every time without fail.

Alfred did so many underwater experiments in that ditch that his father and brothers began making fun of his efforts. Nobel's feelings were hurt but nothing could stop him. He was totally consumed by the challenge of taming nitroglycerin and making it safe for practical use. Finally, he perfected the device so that it would work every time. But as soon as he tried it aboveground, he was back to the same frustrating situation. Sometimes it worked; sometimes it didn't.

Perhaps, Nobel reasoned, the secret was that the

Repauno Dynamite Plant at Gibbstown, New Jersey. This plant became the largest dynamite factory in the world in the 1920s.

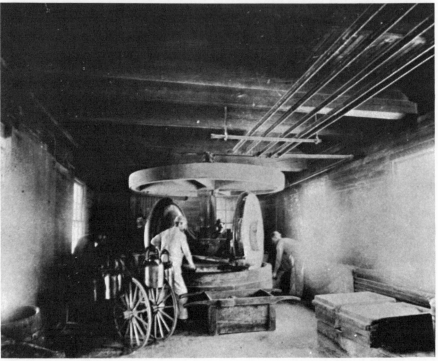

water acted to confine the explosion. He knew shock, not flame, was needed to set off nitroglycerin. Perhaps the gunpowder blast hadn't exerted enough pressure on the glass tube to break it. Nobel decided to close both ends of his powder tube tightly with sealing wax. That would confine the explosion, forcing it to break the glass with enough shock to trigger the oil. It worked beautifully. He had found the answer. Again and again, he was able to detonate the nitroglycerin as consistently aboveground as he had underwater. His father and brothers stopped ridiculing him and became very interested. Alfred was obviously making progress.

Now all he had to do was perfect the device. He made a small cap of tin and filled it with black powder. In doing this he was borrowing the idea of a gun's percussion cap, which had been invented by a Scottish minister who loved to hunt. The minister used the cap to fire his gunpowder charge. Nobel was the first to apply this idea to the field of explosives. The device was a refinement of his original concept of using one kind of explosive to explode another. The idea is called the "primary charge" or the "initial ignition principle." Later, he found better results by using a copper tube instead of a tin one and by replacing the black powder with nitrated mercury. Using his small but powerful blasting caps, he was finally able to explode nitroglycerin in a safe and predictable way.

Interior of Repauno Dynamite Plant (established in 1880). Photo taken in 1895.

29

Eastern Laboratory, an outgrowth of Repauno Dynamite Plant, where research was carried out on dynamite, blasting supplies, and other high explosives.

When 30-year-old Nobel applied for a patent in 1863 to protect this invention, he called it Nobel's Patent Detonator. The idea of using an easily produced explosion to cause the main blast was revolutionary. Later, scientists declared this the most important development in the field of explosives since the invention of gunpowder. Many, in fact, said this principle was of greater value than the later invention of dynamite itself.

Ten years after his blasting cap discovery, Nobel said, "The real era of nitroglycerin opened . . . when a charge of pure nitroglycerin was first set off by means of a minute charge of gunpowder." This was the foundation of the whole modern practice of blasting and all the developments in the field of high explosives that were to follow.

Nobel's invention was immediately put to work. His caps were used to set off large-scale blasting operations in mines owned by a Belgian company. The report of the successful blasts aroused a great deal of interest in 1863. At last the way had been opened to use high explosives in mining, quarrying, and road building that would eventually change the world.

The use of blasting caps meant the world's most violent explosives could be controlled. Or did it? The problem of how to safely manufacture and handle nitroglycerin remained. Alfred Nobel had to find the solution. Nothing spurred him on more than the tragedy that killed his beloved brother.

Inventing and working with explosives had always been a family affair. From before the time Alfred was born, his father had pots of chemicals smoking on the kitchen stove and in his laboratory. Mr.

Ruins of Rolling Mills after 1889 blast leveled this manufacturing plant for explosives.

TAMPING UP.

Underground workers pack dynamite into boreholes with tamping
pole.

Nobel had as many ideas as he had dreams of fame
and riches, but his wild schemes never seemed to produce results. When Alfred returned from Russia to
Sweden he was as excited as his father about the
fantastic oil they had seen explode in a Russian
laboratory.

Alfred's father thought this would finally turn
the family's financial tide. Surely there would be a
great demand for this new and powerful explosive.
After being turned down by local lenders, Alfred was
able to borrow enough money from a Paris bank to

start a small nitroglycerin factory at Heleneborg, Sweden. His father was convinced that riches lay ahead.

But instead of riches, there was disaster and death. Alfred's younger brother, Oscar Emil, offered to work in the factory until he left for college. This gentle and brilliant young man was killed instantly when the plant exploded with a deafening noise. The building was blown to pieces, then consumed by fire. Neighbors ran into the streets with hatchets and

The trick was to light the dynamite fuse and then run. This method of igniting dynamite was used before safer ways were developed.

FIRE IN THE HOLE BUDDY.

pails of water. But it was no use. The factory was nothing but a pile of flaming rubble. Oscar Emil and a few other workers were dead. No one lived to tell what had happened.

The Nobels could put aside their dreams of wealth, but they could never forget the loss of Oscar Emil. He had been full of promise. Nothing would bring him back to life. Each member of the family had to deal with that fact. Alfred was filled with sorrow. His father never recovered from the shock of losing his son. Several months later he suffered a paralyzing stroke. Some years later he died still tormented by his grief.

To complicate matters, there were other serious problems. The city authorities raised a storm of protest. They had had no idea the "blasting oil" the Nobels were manufacturing was really another name for the dangerous explosive nitroglycerin. The community was stunned by the lives already lost and the potential danger to the rest of its citizens. Police notified Alfred that it was against the law to manufacture explosives within the city limits.

Alfred knew nitroglycerin was safe as long as it was handled properly. His many experiments had proved that fact to him long ago. He moved the factory to a barge on a lake just outside town. Frightened folk in the Swedish countryside referred to the barge as the "death ship." When it floated too near shore, they screamed and threatened Alfred with pitchforks.

The Hoosac Tunnel in western Massachusetts—the first job of this sort that used dynamite and pneumatic rock drills. 1856.

Conditions on the barge were far from ideal. Alfred bundled up in bulky clothes to protect himself from the frigid weather. Working long hours, he carefully filled bottles with blasting oil (nitroglycerin) and made blasting caps one by one. His mind kept working on ways to make nitroglycerin safer. At night he went ashore for supplies.

When he had filled a padded suitcase with blasting caps and bottles of oil, Alfred headed for the mining region of the Harz Mountains. There was a need for his powerful product, but he had to prove it was safe to use. Miners were impressed by his demonstrations. Nitroglycerin was cheaper than gunpowder, would do five times the work and the blasting caps made it predictable. After securing a bank loan, Nobel started a factory in Germany to meet the growing

Dynamite revolutionized transportation. Work in progress on St. Clair River Tunnel for the Grand Trunk Railroad between Michigan and Canada.

demand. Nitroglycerin, labeled as blasting oil, was sealed in cans and sent throughout Europe and around the world.

As if the death of his brother were not enough, Alfred soon found himself facing a series of terrible accidents that were the direct result of his new product. He had gone to a great deal of trouble to show that blasting caps made nitroglycerin safe. Alfred always handled the oil with utmost care and expected others would do the same. Surely they would read the warnings printed on the labels. But some of the peasants who transported cans of nitroglycerin over the Swiss Alps in oxcarts couldn't read. Others had no understanding of the explosive potential of their cargo. When the cans leaked, they used the gooey stuff to oil their boots or even as a substitute for axle grease!

Eventually the casual way blasting oil was handled caught up with the world. In 1865 a German traveler left a box of nitroglycerin in a New York hotel. Several months later a porter dragged the strange smoking box out into the street. Luckily it was Sunday morning and there were not many people around. The box went off like a bomb, badly damaging the hotel and nearby houses. Windows shattered, and bystanders were cut by flying glass. Where the box had been, a four-foot gaping hole had been torn in the pavement.

The manufacturers of gunpowder worried that blasting oil would hurt their sales. They warned there would be accidents, that people would be killed by nitroglycerin. They didn't have to wait long to have all their worst predictions come true.

In 1866 twelve men were killed in Sydney, Australia, when two cases of exploding oil destroyed a complex of warehouses. A steamship with many cans of Nobel's blasting oil in the hold blew up in Panama killing more than sixty and causing a million dollars worth of damage. Ten died when the granite building of Wells, Fargo and Company was ripped apart in San Francisco. According to one newspaper, "Fragments of human flesh, bones and brains were found nearly two blocks distant."

Tales of dreadful accidents began pouring in from all over the world. The worst news of all came

when two of Nobel's factories exploded, killing a number of his own workers. Alfred became known as an enemy of the people. Even his friends turned their backs on him.

The public outcry against the horrors caused by Nobel's blasting oil echoed around the world. Railways and ships refused to accept any more cans of the oil. Warehouses dumped them in the sea. Stringent new laws regulated the manufacture and transporting of the explosive. Some countries made possession of nitroglycerin a crime. In the United States, if a fatal accident resulted from mishandling the lethal substance, the lawbreaker was hanged by the neck until dead.

Alfred and his brother Robert realized that as the oil had aged, impurities left in it caused it to decompose and become highly dangerous. They quickly improved their manufacturing methods. Still, Alfred knew there had to be a safer way to package his product and that he had better find it soon. The world was angry. He was heartsick. Time was running out.

Coal miners used dynamite to dramatically increase their production. 1930.

# 4

# DYNAMITE

*Nitroglycerin Tamed*

NOBEL WORKED all the time, trying one experiment after another. Often he stayed up all night. He had to find a way to make nitroglycerin safe to handle and transport. Perhaps the answer was to combine the oil with some other material, something that wouldn't interfere with the explosive power of the liquid. The awful accidents around the world made the problem an urgent one. But he had long known blasting oil had to be improved. "As early as 1863," he wrote, "I was fully aware of the disadvantages of nitroglycerin in its fluid form."

Alfred experimented with many, many substances. He tried mixing nitroglycerin with gunpowder, guncotton, paper powder, paper pulp, porous silica, sawdust, brick dust, cement, coal, ground charcoal, clay, and gypsum bars. Something was

These photos are of the Ripple Rock-Seymour Narrows Project. Located 120 miles northwest of Vancouver, B.C., Seymour Narrows is part of the inland waterway to Alaska. Ripple Rock was a massive underwater mountain and one of the world's worst navigation hazards. It had wrecked more than 100 ships and taken many lives. Two previous efforts to remove the underwater mountain failed, but this 3-year, $3 million blasting project was a complete success. The tunnel under Seymour Narrows extended to a point under Ripple Rock. A large tube in the ceiling carried air for ventilation. Tracks were for the battery-operated locomotive that hauled out broken rock. The white streak at the top of the photo is a light on the hat of a man walking toward the camera lens.

wrong with each combination. Some became lumpy or gooey. Some wouldn't absorb the nitroglycerin and those that did, failed to explode properly.

Alfred's brother wrote urging him to "give up the damned inventing business as soon as possible because it only brings disappointment." Of course it was disappointing. Alfred agreed. Experiment after experiment brought no progress. Lives had been lost. Damage had been done. The world was clamoring against him. He was accused of doing the devil's work. Always his dead brother was on his mind. He had helped create a gigantic problem. It was time to find the solution. He shut himself in his laboratory and went to work. If there was a safer way to use the power of nitroglycerin, he was determined to find it.

He lost count of his experiments. Almost every day he tried something new. One morning he decided to try the spongy clay that was packed between the cans of blasting oil to keep them from bumping each other in the shipping crates. It seemed like a good idea. There was plenty of it around, and it was cheap since it was found all over northern Germany. It was also light, clean, and had a stable chemical nature. This claylike material, formed over millions of years by huge deposits of fossils, was known as kieselguhr earth. Kieselguhr was so porous it absorbed nitroglycerin like a sponge soaking up water. When it had

Drilling boreholes.

Placing dynamite in borehole.

Wiring dynamite charges.

soaked up three times its weight, it developed a puttylike consistency and became easy to work with.

Alfred could knead it and shape it into sticks just the right size to fit into bore holes. When exploded with a blasting cap, the cartridges proved to have lost little of the original power of blasting oil. They were still twenty times stronger than gunpowder.

Nobel was excited, but there were many more tests to try. He lighted the sticks. They burned but did not explode. He hit them with a hammer, threw them against a stone wall, and dropped them off a cliff. To his delight they were almost impossible to detonate by accident. However, they were reliable. They went off instantly when fired by a blasting cap.

Alfred Nobel had a new product. It needed a new name. Nitroglycerin had a terrible reputation. So did blasting oil. People were, with good reason, scared to death of them. He knew many languages and liked the Greek word *dynamis*, which means power. His combination of nitroglycerin and absorbent earth had plenty of power. Nobel called his invention dynamite.

Alfred's painstaking research had finally paid off. Yet for a long time it was rumored that Nobel had discovered dynamite by accident. According to the story, some blasting oil leaked out of one of the cans into the packing material in the shipping crate. Nobel noticed how well the nitroglycerin was absorbed and decided to try to work with this new puttylike material. It was a good tale, but Nobel denied it was ever true. He said the reason he tried kieselguhr earth was because he was impressed by

Watertight cans of explosives being pushed into place in preparation for the Ripple Rock demolition.

its great bulkiness when dried. He knew it would soak up liquid, and he had been looking for just such an absorbent substance. He said, "Dynamite did not therefore come about by chance, but because from the outset I saw the disadvantage of a fluid explosive and set about finding a means of counteracting this drawback."

Alfred Nobel was a problem solver. Dynamite was a practical solution that formed the basis of a gigantic future explosives industry. But at the time of his invention no one was thinking ahead to the era of the atom. There was work to do. The world had been impatiently awaiting a better way to blast rock. There were canals to be dug and minerals to be mined. Now mountains could be moved!

Alfred and his brother Robert set out for the

Experts crimp a waterproof sealer on the end of a detonating cord that detonates at 20,000 feet per second, causing instantaneous explosion.

Setting off explosion.

mines and quarries of Europe to demonstrate their new product. At last they had convincing evidence that dynamite was safe. Fascinated workers and onlookers stood a good distance away while the Nobels tossed cartridges into a roaring fire and hurled them off mountainsides. They challenged explosives experts to make up their own tests. It soon became evident the brothers had not exaggerated the good qualities of dynamite. Their product was safe, easy to transport and handle, convenient to use, and very reliable. When exploded with a blasting cap, it consistently set off a powerful explosion.

The word got out in a hurry. Dynamite could accomplish huge jobs quickly and with great efficiency. Suddenly, impossible projects were possible. Dreams that had once been wild flights of fantasy could actually come true. The world was hungry for this kind of energy.

Sweden, Norway, Germany, and Britain soon built factories to manufacture the new explosive. But nowhere was the enthusiasm as high as in America. The United States was rapidly industrializing. Dynamite promised to do for mining, transportation, and construction what steam power was already accomplishing for manufacturing.

The first dynamite factory in the United States was erected near the California gold mines in 1868. Twelve years later Du Pont, long the country's largest producer of black powder, began manufacturing Nobel's invention in New Jersey. By the 1920s this plant became the largest dynamite factory in the world.

A freighter enjoys safe passage in the once-perilous straits between Vancouver Island and Maud Island. The demolition of the underwater mountain Ripple Rock provided a channel 50 feet deep at low tide.

Colorado Big Thompson project.

Man alone, even many men working for years and years, could not accomplish what dynamite could in a single moment. The first big job the explosive took on in America was to carve out the mile-long Musconnectcong Tunnel near Easton, Pennsylvania, in 1872. In 1866 40 tons of dynamite thrilled a huge crowd of New Yorkers when a giant explosion removed the rock reefs of the East River's Hell Gate section that had long been blocking the port of New York.

All over the world dynamite was going to work. It quarried marble in the Italian mountains and helped European miners get at minerals locked behind mountains of impenetrable rock. It blasted out the Panama Canal to link the Atlantic and Pacific Oceans.

Americans used the new explosive ingeniously. The sculptor Gutzon Borglum roughed out the massive figures on Mount Rushmore with dynamite. Ten million pounds of dynamite dug out the underground path for the New York subway system. Coal miners using dynamite dramatically increased their production, which helped fuel America's tremendous industrial growth. Every kind of mining benefitted from this tireless mountain breaker. Great deposits of copper, iron, zinc, lead, silver, and gold had been waiting since the beginning of time. With dynamite the country's mineral wealth was at last accessible. No cement was made in the United States until dynamite made it practical to blast quarry rock on a grand scale. Millions and millions of pounds of the explosive went into the construction of the Boulder, Shasta, and Grand Coulee Dams, and they became a source of vast hydroelectric power.

Dynamite revolutionized transportation. It carved out road and railroad beds, opened harbors to shipping, and dug the famous Erie Barge Canal as

Saguenay River in Canada. The current of the stream was too swift to permit construction of coffer dams. Dams were built vertically into the air. Supporting rods were blown away, and dams then settled into position across the stream.

well as many other canals. In six years it blasted ninety-two tunnels through the mountains of the west. Engineers estimated the job would have taken 1000 years without dynamite.

Farmers enlisted the help of the new explosive to remove stumps and boulders, clear fields, drain wet land, and dig irrigation ditches. In lumbering it cracked the tops off trees and broke up log jams.

Dynamite dismantled machinery, razed old buildings, and blasted the foundations for new skyscrapers. It dropped smokestacks and bridges, broke ice jams and loosened dirt so steam shovels could work efficiently. Geologists studied the miniature earthquakes it created to help locate oil deposits. In the 1880s dynamite was given credit for ending a severe drought when 200 pounds of it were slung from a balloon and exploded over New York City.

Few discoveries have changed the world as much as dynamite. Along with steam and electricity, it was responsible for the astonishing material development of America and literally constructed our modern world.

Our present high standard of living is a direct outgrowth of blasting natural resources from the earth with dynamite. Du Pont's laboratory for explosives in Gibbstown, New Jersey, evolved into one of the first industrial laboratories for chemical research in the country. A fantastic array of products

Blasting at the Ouachita River in Arkansas, 1948.

that were the chemical cousins of high explosives emerged. These included plastics, dyes, rayon, nylon, cellophane, photographic film, fertilizers, paints, and varnishes.

Nobel had found a safe way to unleash great energy. Dynamite's strength seemed to have no limits. At one time Roger Bacon had feared the awful de-

Thar she blows! Demolition of an iceberg in Greenland. A Coast Guard cutter became trapped after entering an ice-bound harbor to rescue victims of a landslide. Dynamite was used to open an escape channel to the sea.

structive power of gunpowder. What if he had been able to see the awesome force of dynamite at work? Could anything ever surpass its power?

In 1955 more than 750 million pounds of dynamite were used. In that year almost every commercial blasting operation in the country depended on this explosive. But just as Nobel's invention once replaced gunpowder, other explosives eventually came along to make dynamite obsolete.

Water gels were introduced in the 1950s that proved to be more powerful, cheaper to produce, and safer. It wasn't long before they replaced dynamite on the commercial blasting scene. In 1974 Du Pont announced plans to completely phase out dynamite in favor of a new water gel explosive named "Tovex."

Since 1866, when Alfred Nobel first mixed nitroglycerin with kieselguhr earth to make dynamite, the explosive had been used almost exclusively for peaceful purposes. It modernized our world and set us running down the road of technological progress. Yet we know it was also a step in a continuing quest to invent explosives that are more and more powerful, explosives that have not always been used for the good of humanity.

The history of explosives has been a dynamic story of great change. For millions of years energy was supplied solely by fire, wind, water, and muscle power. Since the invention of gunpowder a thousand years ago, there have been more changes than in all prior time. The inventor of gunpowder trembled in

fear for the fate of his fellow humans and tried to withhold the formula. The inventor of nitroglycerin was reluctant to unleash his frightening exploding oil on an unsuspecting world.

Yet our growing appetite for knowledge and power could not be stalled for long. Explosives have been invented that are capable of greater and greater destruction. The atom bomb seemed like the ultimate weapon until the hydrogen bomb came along. Today the potential for nuclear devastation is commonplace. We have the power to literally blow ourselves off the face of the earth.

Our future depends on the way these powerful tools are put to use. Our survival depends upon wise choices. Are we going to put nuclear energy to work for a better life or will we destroy the planet we call home? We now have the means to blast off into the outer reaches of the universe, to explore stars we cannot even see today. The way we choose to use our awesome powers can mean the difference between the end of human life as we know it or the beginning of an era of fantastic progress and space exploration.

Du Pont's original laboratory for explosives in Gibbstown, New Jersey, evolved into one of the first industrial laboratories for chemical research in the country.

# 5

# THE NOBEL PEACE PRIZES

*Nobel's Gift to Humanity*

ALFRED NOBEL was keenly aware of the destructive capability of explosives. Because of them many people around the globe had lost their lives, including his own factory workers. He could never forget the violent blast that had killed his own brother.

But he never thought of himself as an enemy of humanity. His inventions had been used mainly in constructive ways. He was in awe of the powerful explosives developed in his own lifetime, but his hope was that they would lead ultimately to peace. At one point he wrote, "The day when two army corps will be able to destroy each other in one second, all civilized nations will recoil from war in horror and disband their armies." But he lived long enough to doubt the truth of his prediction. Today we know even though nations can destroy each other in a second,

A fantastic array of products was developed as a result of research in the area of explosives. These products (all chemical cousins of high explosives) included rayon, nylon, plastics, dyes, cellophane, photographic film, fertilizers, paints, and varnishes.

they still have armies and they still go to war.

As Alfred neared the end of his life, he was filled with grief when given the news his brother, Ludwig, had died. He suffered an additional blow when he read the newspaper obituary. The paper had confused the two brothers and had written about Alfred instead of Ludwig. It summed up Alfred's life by calling him "the merchant of death." Nobel couldn't believe it. So this was what the world thought of him and his inventions, nothing more than instruments of death and destruction.

Nobel vowed to set the record straight, to clear the Nobel name. All his life he had struggled for the betterment of the human race. But what could he do to prove it at this late date?

Alfred Nobel was one of the richest men of his time. He spent a great deal of time searching his soul for the best way to dispose of this immense fortune. After reading the newspaper clipping about his life, he began rewriting his will. He declared that all his wealth should go into a trust fund that would administer the Nobel Peace Prizes. These awards would be given each year to those who had done the most to benefit humanity and to promote the cause of world peace. Because Nobel had always considered himself a citizen of the world rather than of just one country, he gave strict instructions that candidates of every nationality be given an equal chance to win.

When he finished writing his will he knew he had done the best he could. Nobel had used everything he had—his intelligence, his wisdom, his compassion, and the fortune that dynamite had created. This very practical man with an intense interest in peace had at last done something about it.

Alfred Nobel died in 1896, a lonely, unhappy man fearing the future for his fellow human beings. Today when we remember him, it is appropriate that we associate his name with our continuing search for peace. Alfred Nobel might be surprised to know the world-famous Nobel Peace Prizes have outlasted the era of dynamite.

# INDEX

Accidents, 36–39
  at Nobel's factories, 33–34,
    39
Arabs, gunpowder used by,
    10–11
Arkansas, 52
Arrows shot by gunpowder, 11
Atom bomb, 57
Australia, accident in, 37

Bacon, Roger, black powder
    formula of, 11–12, 16,
    54–55
Big Thompson project
    (Colorado), 49
Black powder, see Gunpowder
Blasting caps
  for dynamite, 44
  for nitroglycerin, 29–31
Blasting oil, see Nitroglycerin
Borglum, Gutzon, 50
Boston Massacre (1770), 19
Brimstone, 11
Britain, 48

Canada, 36, 50
  Ripple Rock–Seymour
    Narrows Project in, 41,
    45, 48
Carlyle, Thomas, 15
Castles, gunpowder and
    history of, 13, 14
Cement, dynamite and
    manufacture of, 50

China, invention of fireworks
    in, 9–10
Coal mining, 38, 50
Coast Guard cutter freed from
    ice, 54
Colorado, 49

Dams, dynamite in
    construction of, 50–51
Democracy, gunpowder and
    rise of, 12–15
Detonating cord, 46, 47
Du Pont
  laboratory of, 30, 53–54, 57,
    59
  new "Tovex" explosive of, 55
  Repauno Dynamite Plant
    of, 27–30, 48, 53
Dynamite
  detonating cord for, 46, 47
  drilling boreholes for, 42
  ignition of, 33
  naming of, 45
  new explosive to replace, 55
  Nobel's invention of, 16–18,
    40–47
  plants for, 27–30, 48, 53
  tamping of, 32
  in tunneling, 35, 36, 49, 53
  wiring of, 44

Eastern Laboratory
    (Gibbstown, New Jersey),
    30, 53–54, 57, 59

Easton (Pennsylvania), 49
Erie Barge Canal, 50

Farmers, dynamite used by,
    53
Fireworks, Chinese, 9–10

Germany, 35, 48
Gibbstown (New Jersey),
    dynamite plant in,
    27–30, 48, 53
Glycerin, 18
Grand Trunk Railroad, 36
Greek fire, 11
Greenland, 54
Gunpowder (black powder),
    9–15
  Nobel's experiments with,
    26–29, 40
  in Revolutionary War, 20
  in tunneling, 17

Harz Mountains (Germany),
    35
Heleneborg (Sweden), 33–34
Hell Gate (New York City), 49
Hoosac Tunnel
    (Massachusetts), 35
Hydrogen bomb, 57

Iceberg, demolition of, 54
Initial ignition principle, 29
Italy, 50

Kieselguhr, 43–46
Knights in armor, gunpowder
    and history of, 13–15

*Maine* (battleship), 13
Massachusetts, 35
Mercury, nitrated, 29
Michigan, 36
Mining
    dynamite in, 32, 33, 38, 50

gunpowder in, 15
nitroglycerin in, 31
Mount Rushmore sculpture,
    50
Musconnectcong Tunnel
    Pennsylvania), 49

New Jersey, Repauno
    Dynamite Plant in,
    27–30, 48, 53
New York City
    dynamite exploded over, 53
    Hell Gate, 49
    nitroglycerin blast in
    (1865), 37
    subways in, 50
New York State, Erie Barge
    Canal in, 50
Nitrated mercury, 29
Nitric acid, 18
Nitroglycerin (blasting oil),
    16–21
  accidents with, 33–34,
    36–39
  effect of aging on, 39
  Nobel's barge factory for,
    34–35
  Nobel's detonator for,
    25–31, 35
Nobel, Alfred, 9
  accidents in factories of,
    33–34, 39
  called "merchant of death,"
    59–60
  childhood and education of,
    22–24
  death of, 60
  dynamite invented by,
    16–18, 40–47
  father of, 22–23, 27, 31–34
  mother of, 22–24
  nitroglycerin barge factory
    of, 34–35

63

nitroglycerin detonator
 invented by, 25–31, 35
 peace prizes of, 58–61
 portrait of, 26
 woman companion of,
 24–25

Nobel, Ludwig, 24, 59
Nobel, Oscar Emil, 24
 death of, 31–34, 58
Nobel, Robert, 24, 39, 46
Nobel Peace Prizes, 58–61
Nobel's Patent Detonator, 30
Norway, 48
Nuclear energy, 57

Oil deposits, locating, 53
Ouachita River, 53

Panama, accident in, 37
Panama Canal, 50
Peace, Nobel and, 58–61
Pennsylvania, 49
Primary charge, 29

Rainmaking, New York City's
 use of dynamite for, 53
Repauno Dynamite Plant (Du
 Pont), 27–30, 48, 53
Revolutionary War, black
 powder in, 20
Ripple Rock–Seymour
 Narrows Project, 41, 45,
 48
Rolling Mills, ruins of, 31
Russia, Nobel in, 23, 25, 32

Saguenay River, 50
St. Clair River Tunnel, 36
Saltpeter, 11
 refinery for, 23, 24

San Francisco, accident in, 37
Sculpture, dynamite used for,
 50
Sobrero, Ascanio,
 nitroglycerin invented by,
 18–21
Stockholm (Sweden), 22
Sulfuric acid, 18
Sulfur, 11
Sweden
 dynamite factories in, 48
 Nobel's birth and childhood
 in, 22–24
Sydney (Australia), 37

"Tovex," 55
Transportation, dynamite
 and, 50–53
Tunneling
 black powder used in, 17
 dynamite used in, 35, 36,
 49, 53

Underwater explosions
 greatest, 10
 See also Ripple Rock–
 Seymour Narrows Project
United States, dynamite
 factories in, 27–30, 48, 53

Vancouver Island, see Ripple
 Rock–Seymour Narrows
 Project

War
 gunpowder's change of
 nature of, 12–15
 Nobel and, 58–61
Water gels, 55
Wells, Fargo and Company, 37
Wildfire, Greek, 11